DATE DUE

398.2

Hughes $10.00

AUTHOR

The Months of the Year

TITLE

DATE DUE	BORROWER'S NAME	ROOM NUMBER
DEC 1 6 199	Whitehill	D1(4)
AR 0 6	Ashley	D39
MAR 1 8 1998	Clecia A.	B454

398.2
Hughes
The Months of the
Year

THE MONTHS OF THE YEAR

Text © copyright 1989 by Garrett Educational Corporation
First published in the United States in 1989 by
Garrett Educational Corporation, 130 East 13th Street,
Ada, OK 74820
First published by Young Library Ltd., Brighton, England
© Copyright 1982 Young Library Ltd.

Manufactured in the United States of America

Library of Congress Cataloging in Publication Data

Hughes, Paul.
  The months of the year: stories, songs, traditions, festivals,
and surprising facts about the months of the year all over the world
/ Paul Hughes.
      p. cm.
    Bibliography: p.
    Includes index.
    Summary: Presents a variety of facts, stories, songs, festivals,
and traditions about the months of the year from all over the world.
    1. Months—Folklore—Juvenile literature.   2. Calendar—Folklore—
Juvenile literature.   [1. Months—Folklore.   2. Calendar—
Folklore.]   I. Title.
GR930.H85   1989
398.27—dc20   89-11759
    ISBN 0-944483-33-X   CIP
                                                       AC

THE MONTHS OF THE YEAR

A year is twelve months — but what *is* a month? Why thirty days hath September? Have you ever wondered why January is called January, or July is called July? Why do people dance around maypoles in May, or send each other Valentine cards in February, or eat turkey at Thanksgiving in November? And why do Jews, Moslems, and Hindus seem to hold so many festivals at the same time as Christians? You can read about all these things here, and also learn lots of rhymes and sayings about the months, and discover the names of the months in more than a hundred countries all over the world.

People can have different ideas about customs, rhymes, and sayings handed down by word of mouth or translated from other languages. Also, people do not always agree about facts in legend and history. Therefore, you should expect to read slightly different versions of these things in other books.

THE MONTHS

Written by PAUL HUGHES

OF THE YEAR

Illustrated by JEFFREY BURN

GEC GARRETT EDUCATIONAL CORPORATION

Contents

New moon

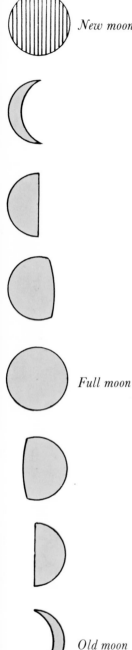

New moon

Full moon

Old moon

What is a month?

New moons and old moons

Here is an old Indian riddle. See if you can solve it.

> *What has two horns when young,*
> *Loses them in middle age,*
> *And regains them in old age?*

The answer is — the moon. Have you noticed how the shape of the moon changes each night? Sometimes it is a thin, silver crescent (called the new moon). Then it grows a little bit larger and rounder each night until it forms a complete circle (the full moon). The next night it starts getting smaller again until it is a crescent once more (the old moon). Then it actually disappears altogether for a night, before reappearing as another new moon.

The two ends of the crescent are the "horns" mentioned in the Indian riddle.

Lunar years

Thousands of years ago, people measured their year by the changing of the moon. They noticed that the moon changed from new to old and back to new again about every 29½ days. They called this period by a name that meant moon — a month. There were roughly twelve of them each year.

These people thought the moon changed shape because it was magical, so they worshipped it. Now we know the real reason. The moon goes around and around the earth, while the earth goes around and around the sun. The moon and the earth are constantly changing places; some-

8

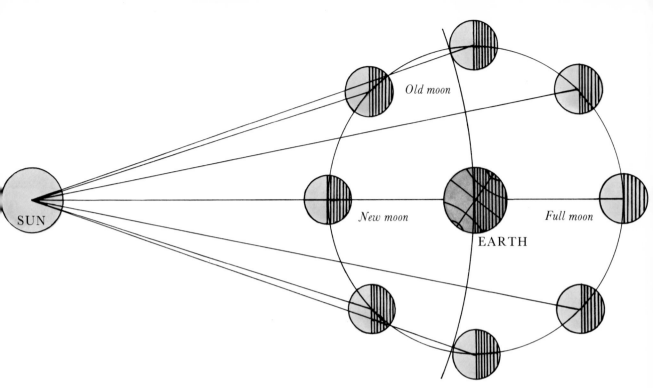

Old moon

New moon

Full moon

SUN

EARTH

times the earth is between the sun and the moon, and sometimes the moon is between the sun and the earth.

We could not see the moon at all if the sun did not shine on it. The moon shines by reflecting the light from the sun like a giant mirror in the sky. However, from our position on the earth we often cannot see the whole of the part which is lit up. The diagram above shows how a part of the moon remains in darkness, and invisible, if we cannot see the light reflected from it. The size and shape of the visible part is different each night.

When early man began to make up calendars to measure the passing of time, he thought of a year as twelve months. As a month was about 29½ days, he made some months of 29 days and some of 30 days so that they would average 29½ days. This year of twelve months is called a lunar year. Lunar means moon, so a lunar year is a year measured by the passing of twelve moons (months). The lunar year is 354 days (12 × 29½ days).

Solar years

There is another way of measuring a year — by counting the number of days that it takes the earth to make one orbit of the sun. In that time we see the seasons pass from spring to summer, summer to autumn, autumn to winter, and back again to spring. Most people say that this covers 365 days, and they are almost right. But they are not *exactly* right. In fact it takes 365.242199 days! This period — the exact time it takes for the earth to travel around the sun — is called a solar year. Solar means sun.

In ancient times, people who used the lunar calendar found that it was out of step with the solar year, and it got further out of step as the years went by. The ancient Romans began to notice that their spring festivals were taking place further back into the winter.

The Julian calendar

The Roman civilization (of about 2,000 years ago) was a very powerful one that colonized most of Europe. We are very interested in the Roman calendar, because it is the one we use today (with just a few changes).

Until about 2,000 years ago the Romans used the lunar calendar. When they realized that their calendar was out of step with the seasons, they decided to change it. Julius Caesar, the great leader of the Romans, abolished the old lunar calendar and introduced a new one based on the solar year. He realized that each year had about 365 days

6 hours. Six hours is a quarter of a day. So Julius Caesar decided to add to 365 days one extra day every four years, making the average year 365¼ days. The first three years were 365 days each, and the fourth year had two 23rds of February. This fourth year, with its extra day, was called a leap year. The year began in March and the months were arranged like this:

1	Martius, 31 days	7	September, 31 days
2	Aprilus, 30 days	8	October, 30 days
3	Maius, 31 days	9	November, 31 days
4	Junius, 30 days	10	December, 30 days
5	Julius, 31 days	11	Januarius, 31 days
6	Sextilis, 30 days	12	Februarius, 29 or 30 days

Later in the book we tell you how these months got their names, but we will just mention here that the fifth month was named in honor of Julius Caesar himself.

The next Roman leader was Augustus Caesar, and he decided to make a few more changes. One reason was that he too wanted a month named in honor of himself. So he changed Sextilis to Augustus; and, because Julius's month had 31 days, gave Augustus an extra day so that it would not be shorter than Julius. That extra day was taken from Februarius. To keep close to the orderly arrangement of alternate months of 30 and 31 days, he then cut September and November to 30 days and increased October and December to 31 days.

So now the calendar looked like this:

1	Martius, 31 days	7	September, 30 days
2	Aprilus, 30 days	8	October, 31 days
3	Maius, 31 days	9	November, 30 days
4	Junius, 30 days	10	December, 31 days
5	Julius, 31 days	11	Januarius, 31 days
6	Augustus, 31 days	12	Februarius, 28 or 29 days

11

The spellings have changed slightly. Otherwise these are the names, and the number of days, which are still used today in most European and Christian countries of the world.

However, even the Julian and Augustan calendars were not quite right, because there are not *exactly* 365 days 6 hours in a solar year. Now that we have great telescopes and other scientific instruments, we know that a year is 365 days, 5 hours, 48 minutes, and 49.7 seconds! The Julian and Augustan calendars were slightly too long. This was not noticeable at first, for no one cared about gaining 11 minutes, 10.3 seconds each year. However, as the centuries passed by, every year gained those few extra minutes. By the sixteenth century the calendar was wrong by 10 days.

The Gregorian calendar

In 1583 Pope Gregory announced a new calendar, to sort out those extra few minutes each year. First he ordered that October 5 of that year should be reckoned as the 15th (which worried a lot of people who thought their lives would therefore be ten days shorter!). That brought the calendar back to its proper place again. Then he said that the leap year should be left out three times in every four centuries, during the centenary year. This is how it works:

    1600, a leap year
    1700, 1800, 1900, not leap years
    2000, a leap year
    2100, 2200, 2300, not leap years
    2400, a leap year
        and so on.

The Gregorian calendar is wrong by only one day in 3,323 years. Later another change was made to the calen-

12

dar and now it is wrong by only one day in 20,000 years. That should be accurate enough to satisfy most people.

Pope Gregory wanted all Christian countries to adopt his calendar immediately, but they did not. All the Catholic countries followed Gregory's example, but Britain did not adopt it until 1752 and other countries were later still.

Now many non-Christian countries use the calendar which has come down to us from Julius Caesar and Pope Gregory. It is the official calendar in most countries of the world, although some still use the lunar calendar for religious affairs.

Here is an old rhyme to help you remember the number of days in each month.

> *Thirty days hath September,*
> *April, June, and November;*
> *All the rest have thirty-one,*
> *Except for February alone,*
> *Which has but twenty-eight days clear,*
> *And twenty-nine in each leap year.*

13

January

Janus's month

January is the first month of the year and is thirty-one days long. The name of January comes from the Roman god Janus. Janus had two faces; this allowed him to look both backwards into the old year and forwards into the new one at the same time. He was the "spirit of opening." The Romans always had a special thought for him when they were opening a new building or at the opening of a new day, month, or year.

In the very earliest Roman calendars there were no months of January or February at all. To the Romans, ten was a very important number. It seemed right that ten should be the number of months in a year. So their year was made up of ten months, with just a gap between the end of December and the new year, which began in March. Even when January (or Januarius as the Romans called it) was added, the new year continued to start in March. It remained so in England and its colonies until about 200 years ago.

Wolf month

The Anglo-Saxons called January *Wulf monath*, which means wolf month. At this time of year, cold and hunger forced packs of wolves to enter towns and villages in search of food. During the reign of Queen Elizabeth I, the name of the month became Ianuary or Januar. By the time the first colonies were being set up in America at the end of the seventeenth century, the name had changed to the one we know today. In Victorian times, however, some people called the month Janiveer, as this old proverb shows:

The blackest month of all the year,
Is the month of Janiveer.

In the Northern Hemisphere, January is often the coldest month of the year. For most people long ago it was a very hard time indeed, and there are many old proverbs and sayings about the weather during January. Even if the January weather was mild, people expected it to get worse later on, as this Italian proverb tells:

If January stays in his shirtsleeves (is mild)
March will explode with laughter (will mock you with bad weather).

New Year all over the world

January is not all misery and gloom, however. It is the first month of the New Year, so is greeted with celebrations and merrymaking in countries all over the world. Usually these festivities last only a day or so, but the Chinese New Year celebrations last for two weeks. They start with the new moon between January 21 and February 19, and continue until the full moon. In Hong Kong, Tibet, Malaysia, and in the Chinese quarters of cities around the world, colorful floats, lanterns, and paper dragons fill the streets.

Around the middle of January, the Hindus celebrate the festival of Makar Sankranti. They bathe and rub them-

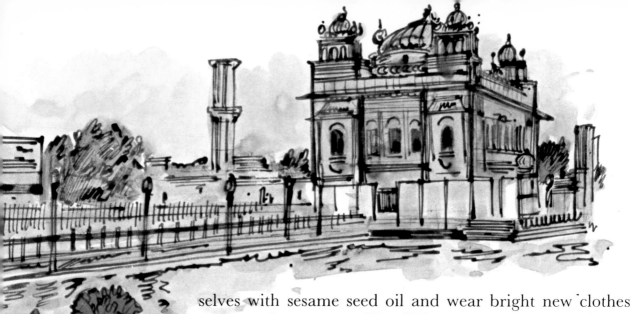

selves with sesame seed oil and wear bright new clothes and lots of ornaments. The Sikhs, a separate group of Hindus, celebrate the birthday of one of their great leaders, Guru Gobind Singh, with special services in their temples.

On January 6, Christians celebrate Twelfth Night or Epiphany — the night when the three wise men arrived to see the baby Jesus. Members of the Greek and Russian Orthodox churches celebrate Christmas around this time, because they still use the Julian calendar, which is now thirteen days behind the Gregorian. In Greece, people bless a glass of water and carry basil sprigs around with them. They believe that this will ward off the *kalikangare* — goblins who come up from the middle of the earth to roam around.

January 1 marks Lincoln's 1863 Emancipation Proclamation freeing slaves in the South — formalized in Texas on June 19, 1865, and celebrated as "Juneteenth," a Texas holiday. The third Monday in January honors Dr. Martin Luther King, a famous black civil rights leader who was assassinated.

If your birthday is in January, your lucky flowers are carnations and snowdrops, and your lucky stone is the garnet.

February

Februus's month

February usually has 28 days, but every fourth year it has 29 days. Februus was the Roman god of purification, or cleansing. The name February either comes from him, or from a musical instrument called a februa. The februa was played during the Roman festivals of Februar, Feralia, and Lupercalia, all held around this time of the year. Lupercalia was a very romantic occasion. Even today February 14 is celebrated as St. Valentine's Day, a day for lovers when young men and women send each other cards with loving rhymes printed on them.

The Anglo-Saxons had two names for February. They called it *Kale monath* because kale, a plant rather like cabbage, was their main source of food in that bleak month. They also named it *Lenet monath* (lengthening month); in the Northern Hemisphere the days begin to get longer around this time. The word "Lent" comes from "lenet."

In Shakespeare's time about 400 years ago, the second month of the year was called Feverell. One hundred years later it had become Februeer. The modern name, February, is only about a hundred years old.

Americans show a sense of humor by observing Groundhog Day on February 2. They also observe the birthdays of presidents Lincoln on February 12 and Washington on February 22.

Looking forward to spring

In the cooler countries of the Northern Hemisphere, the weather is still very dreary in February. Most of the old proverbs seem to suggest that the more awful the weather

17

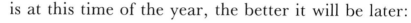

is at this time of the year, the better it will be later:

If February give much snow,
A fine summer it doth foreshow.

If you go around with a "February face," then you are very miserable indeed. Some people can always find cause for optimism, however, as this old Arabic proverb suggests:

Though February storms and blusters,
It has the smell of summer in it.

The Japanese mark the end of the winter with a bean-throwing ceremony. During the winter in the far north, it is dark all day for some of the winter months. So in Norway they celebrate the return of the sun after the long period of winter darkness.

February festivals

Christians all over the world celebrate Lent, when they give up certain foods for a period of forty days. This is to commemorate the forty days and nights that Christ spent without food in the wilderness.

At this time of year Jewish people celebrate Tu B'shvat, the new year for trees. For every girl baby born on the first day of the new year, a cypress tree is planted. For every boy baby it is a cedar tree. When the children

18

grow up, the trees are cut down and made into their marriage canopy.

The Malagasy, who live on the island of Madagascar, are very superstitious about February. They believe that if a child is born on the first day of the month, their house will burn down. So they build a little hut and set fire to it with mother and baby inside. The curse is broken when the two of them run out screaming.

Hindus celebrate Sri Ramakrishna's birthday. He was a Hindu saint who lived in the nineteenth century. Around the middle or end of the month they hold the festival of Maha-sivaratri — the night of the great Siva. Siva is one of the Hindu forms of God. On the blackest night of the month, He is worshipped with flowers all night.

If there are 29 days in this month, it is part of a leap year. A leap year is every fourth year, which has an extra day in February — February 29. There is a very old custom that in leap years a woman may ask a man to marry her, instead of waiting to be asked as is the usual custom. It was actually a law in some countries, including Scotland and France. If a man refused, he had to pay a penalty.

If you were born in February, your lucky flowers are primroses and violets; your lucky gemstone is the amethyst.

19

March

Mars's month

The third month of the year is thirty-one days long and is named after Mars. Mars was the Roman god of war, crops, and vegetation. Although it is now the third month of the year, in the old Roman calendar it used to be the first. It was the first month in Britain until 1752. Even now, March 21 is New Year's Day in Iran and other parts of the Middle East.

The Anglo-Saxons called the month *Hlyd monath,* which means stormy month, or *Hraed monath,* which means rugged month. During the Middle Ages it was called Mearch, Mars, or Marche. One of the first times that the name March appears is in a play by William Shakespeare called *Julius Caesar.* Caesar is warned by a fortune-teller that there is a plot to kill him. The fortune-teller says, "Beware the ides of March." (The ides are a Roman division of time and fall about the middle of each month.)

March madness

In many countries of the Northern Hemisphere, March is a time of changeable weather. But by the end of the month the conditions begin to improve and spring has arrived. The winds drop, and animals and plants begin to stir. As the saying goes:

> *March comes in like a lion,*
> *But goes out like a lamb.*

Both animals and people seem to do strange things in March. Have you ever been called "mad as a March hare?" Hares do tend to become a little shy and wild in

March, because it is their mating season. In Lewis Carroll's book *Alice in Wonderland*, there was a mad March hare at the Hatter's tea party.

March festivals

Hindu people of India have a strange festival around March time. It is called Holi and is rather like April Fools' Day (see page 23). The day is spent sending people on pointless errands, poking fun at grown-ups, and squirting or throwing red and yellow powder.

St. Patrick's Day, March 17, is an Irish holiday remembering the Irish saint who, by legend, rid Ireland of snakes. American Irish wear green to celebrate this day.

Jewish people celebrate Purim, in memory of the day when the Jewish Queen Esther saved the Jews from their enemy Haman. At Purim pageants, plays of the story are acted and pastries called ''Haman's ear'' are eaten. In Japan, a doll festival is held in March in honor of all the children's dolls in that country. In Melbourne, Australia, there is the Moomba Festival. Moomba is an old Australian aborigine word. It means something like ''let's get together and enjoy ourselves,'' and that is exactly what the people of Melbourne do. There are carnivals, music and songs, and dazzling firework displays.

If you were born in March, your lucky flowers are daffodils; your lucky gemstones, the bloodstone and aquamarine.

April

The opening month

April is thirty days long and is the fourth month of the year. No one knows for certain how it got its name, but it may have come from "aperire." *Aperire* is a Latin word (the language the Romans used to speak) and means "to open." April is, after all, the month when in the Northern Hemisphere buds begin to open and things start to grow again after the winter.

Eostre monath or *Eastremonath* was the Anglo-Saxon name for the month. The name of the Christian festival of Easter comes from this Anglo-Saxon word. Before the present spelling of April was used it was often spelled Averill. If you look at the chart on page 44, you will see that French people still use a "v" in the spelling.

April song

There is an old legend that three days were taken from April and given to March. However, it appears to have brought the month no good at all:

> *March borrowed from Averill,*
> *Three days and they were ill,*
> *The one was sleet, and the other was snow,*
> *And the third was the worst that ever did blow.*

In the cool countries of the Northern Hemisphere, April is the month when spring weather arrives. In Britain, particularly, people feel a special happiness at the beauty of spring. Robert Browning, an English poet who lived around 150 years ago, longed to be in England even when he was living in the much warmer country of Italy.

Oh to be in England,
Now that April's there.

April is also the month when many migrating birds return from southern habitats, as this rhyme tells us:

Cuckoo, cuckoo, what do you do?
In April come I will,
In May I sing all day,
In June I change my tune,
In July I prepare to fly,
In August go I must.

April festivals

The very first day of April brings All Fools' Day, sometimes called April Fool's Day. It is the custom to play tricks on people, send them on false errands, or make them believe in an impossible story. No one really knows where this custom came from, but it is very old. People were doing it 400 years ago in France. Now it is practiced all over Europe and in other countries around the world. Anyone successfully tricked is called an April Fool. In Scotland such a person is called a gowk, which means

cuckoo. The day Hindus called Holi is quite similar (see March).

April is very important for Christians because Holy Week usually falls in this month. This is to commemorate Christ's triumphant entry into Jerusalem, his betrayal, and his death on the cross. Other religions have important festivals around this time, too. For Jewish people it is the time of Passover, which commemorates the Jews' escape from Egypt. The custom of spring cleaning probably comes from the Jewish rule that all houses must be clean and tidy before the Passover feasting may begin.

Around this time of year, Buddhists celebrate the birth of Lord Buddha, the founder of their religion. In Japan, statues of the Buddha are bathed with hydrangea leaf tea. Sikhs honor the day when Guru Gobind Singh baptized his first five disciples. The ceremony by which people can be baptized into the Sikh faith is known as Amrit. In the Chinese calendar there is the festival of Ching Ming. At Ching Ming all must go and visit the graves of their ancestors and offer them flowers.

If you were born in April, your lucky flowers are the sweet pea and the daisy; your lucky gemstone is the diamond.

May

Maia's month

May, the fifth month of the year, is thirty-one days long. Its name probably comes either from the Greek goddess Maia or from Maia majesta, an Italian goddess of spring. People made sacrifices to Maia majesta in Roman times to ensure growth of their crops. The month is a time of great celebration in the Northern Hemisphere. It is the time when flowers emerge and crops begin to sprout.

The first day of May, called May Day, is celebrated in many parts of the world by dancing around a maypole. In Sweden, boys representing winter and summer hold a mock battle in which summer always wins. In Italy it is celebrated by young people collecting boughs to decorate the front doors of relatives and friends. The first day of May has for centuries been a special day in many countries.

The Anglo-Saxons called the month Thrimilce (three times milking) because cows feeding on the lush May grass could be milked three times a day. It was first called May in about 1430. Before then it was called Maius, Mayes, or Mai. Mai is still the spelling used in French, German, and Welsh (see chart on pages 44 and 45).

The unlucky month

Although the month begins with jolly May Day celebrations, in England May is believed to be an unlucky month, particularly for marriages. As this old saying tells:

Marry in May and you'll rue the day.

25

The French, however, think that May is the month for romance and believe that:

He has a very hard heart that does not love in May.

Many strange beliefs are attached to May. In Britain and the rest of Europe, bathing in dew collected fresh on the first day of May was supposed to ensure lasting beauty. But never buy a broom in May or wash blankets:

Wash a blanket in May,
Wash a dear one away.

For Christians May brings Holy Thursday, also called Ascension Day. Ascension Day is always forty days after Easter, and commemorates the day that Christ ascended into heaven. It is said that the weather should always be fine on this day as it is the day Jesus "kissed the clouds."

Mexicans and Mexican-Americans celebrate May 5, *Cinco de Mayo,* in honor of Mexico's defeat of an invading French force on May 5, 1862. Americans celebrate Mother's Day on the second Sunday in May. At month's end, Americans also honor their war dead by observing Memorial Day, officially May 30.

If you were born in May, your lucky flowers are lilies of the valley and your lucky gemstone is the emerald.

Nuts in May

If you would like to revive a traditional game for the first day of May, try this one. It's called "Here we go gathering nuts in May," although it should really be "knots" in May, because those are the original words. On the first of May long ago people used to gather knots (bouquets) of flowers on May Day.

The game can be played inside or out, and you really need at least ten people. First you must form two equal groups and stand in lines facing each other. Between the

groups, draw a line down the middle on the ground or drop a handkerchief to mark the center.

Now one team joins hands and walks up to the center line and back again, singing:

> *Here we go gathering nuts in May,*
> *Nuts in May, nuts in May,*
> *Here we go gathering nuts in May,*
> *On a cold and frosty morning.*

Then the other team joins hands and walks to the center line and back, singing:

> *Whom will you have for nuts in May,*
> *Nuts in May, nuts in May,*
> *Whom will you have for nuts in May,*
> *On a cold and frosty morning?*

The first team then decides whom it will have from the opposing team, and sings:

> *We will have _____ for nuts in May,*
> *Nuts in May, nuts in May,*
> *We will have _____ for nuts in May,*
> *On a cold and frosty morning.*

The other team then sings:

And whom will you have to fetch him (or her) away,
Fetch him away, fetch him away,
Whom will you have to fetch him away,
On a cold and frosty morning?

The first team then decides on someone who is about the same size as the member they have gained, and sings:

We will have _____ to fetch him (or her) away,
Fetch him away, fetch him away,
We will have _____ to fetch him away,
On a cold and frosty morning.

The two chosen members then have a tug-of-war across the center line. The first one to be pulled over that mark has to join the opposing team. The game goes on until one team has no one left, or everyone is too tired!

28

June

Juno's month

June is the sixth month of the year. It has thirty days and marks the beginning of the summer in the countries of the Northern Hemisphere. Its name is believed to come either from Junius, which was the name of an old Roman tribe, or from Juno. Juno was the chief of all the Roman goddesses. It was her job to look after the interests of Roman women. For this reason, June has always been looked upon as the best month in which to marry:

> *Married in the month of roses — June*
> *Life will be one long honeymoon.*

Sera monath (dry month) was the name the Anglo-Saxons gave to the month. By the time of William Caxton (the first printer of a book in England, in 1475) the name had become Iunius or Iuyn. In William Shakespeare's plays it is called Iune. It was first called June about 200 years ago, in the time of George Washington and Captain James Cook.

The beginning of summer

In the Northern Hemisphere, June is the month of bright flowers and the growth of trees and crops:

> *Calm weather in June,*
> *Sets corn in tune.*

In America there are lots of special names given to animals and plants that appear in June. The June berry is the fruit of a small tree called the Shad bush. June grass is

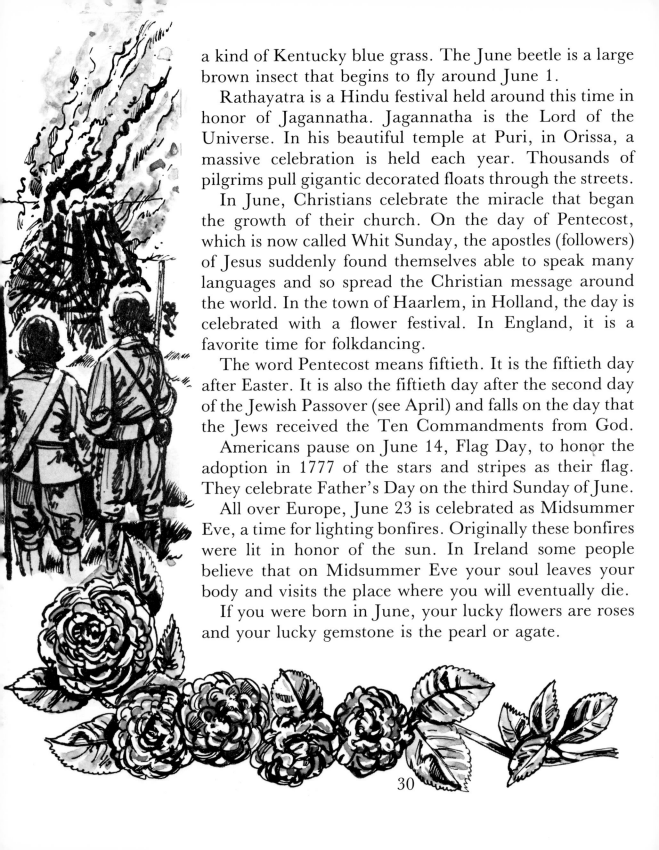

a kind of Kentucky blue grass. The June beetle is a large brown insect that begins to fly around June 1.

Rathayatra is a Hindu festival held around this time in honor of Jagannatha. Jagannatha is the Lord of the Universe. In his beautiful temple at Puri, in Orissa, a massive celebration is held each year. Thousands of pilgrims pull gigantic decorated floats through the streets.

In June, Christians celebrate the miracle that began the growth of their church. On the day of Pentecost, which is now called Whit Sunday, the apostles (followers) of Jesus suddenly found themselves able to speak many languages and so spread the Christian message around the world. In the town of Haarlem, in Holland, the day is celebrated with a flower festival. In England, it is a favorite time for folkdancing.

The word Pentecost means fiftieth. It is the fiftieth day after Easter. It is also the fiftieth day after the second day of the Jewish Passover (see April) and falls on the day that the Jews received the Ten Commandments from God.

Americans pause on June 14, Flag Day, to honor the adoption in 1777 of the stars and stripes as their flag. They celebrate Father's Day on the third Sunday of June.

All over Europe, June 23 is celebrated as Midsummer Eve, a time for lighting bonfires. Originally these bonfires were lit in honor of the sun. In Ireland some people believe that on Midsummer Eve your soul leaves your body and visits the place where you will eventually die.

If you were born in June, your lucky flowers are roses and your lucky gemstone is the pearl or agate.

July

Julius Caesar's month

July is the seventh month of the year and is thirty-one days long. In the early Roman calendar it was called Quintilius. "Quin" is the Latin for five, as in "quintet." July was the fifth month because the Roman calendar began in March. The name was changed to Julius in honor of Julius Caesar because he was born at that time of the year.

The Anglo-Saxons had three names for July. They called it *Maedd monath*, which means meadow month, because it was the time when meadows were at their richest. They also called it *Hey monath* because it was the time of the hay harvest; and *Lida Aefter,* which means second mild month. Through the centuries the name of the month was known as Julio, Iuyl, and Iule. It became July soon after the Great Fire of London in 1666, although for a long time after it was pronounced to rhyme with truly.

Forty days of rain

July 15 is St. Swithun's day. Swithun was a Bishop of Winchester, in England, who lived around 1,100 years ago. After he had been dead and buried for 200 years, the monks of Winchester decided to try and move his bones into the cathedral. But the Saint was so annoyed by this that he commanded it to rain, and it did! In fact, it rained so much that his coffin got stuck in the mud and eventually the monks let him be. From then until now it has always been said that:

> *St. Swithun's day, if thou dost rain,*
> *For forty days it will remain,*

31

*St. Swithun's day, if thou be fair,
For forty days 'twill rain nae mair.*

King Louis-Philippe of France was called the July Monarch because he came to the throne after the July Revolution, which took place on July 27-29, 1830. There is also a flower which bears the name of the month — the July flower — although this is believed to have come from its original name, which was the gillyflower.

In Japan the Bon Festival (the Feast of the Dead) is held. Families put out colored lanterns to light the way home for dead ancestors, and dances are held under the full moon. Also under the the full moon at this time, Hindus celebrate Rakshabandhan, or Rakhi, which means a tie. On this day girls tie colorful bands of cotton or silk on their brothers' wrists. This symbolizes the tie between brother and sister and the protection that the brother must give. In the United States, Americans celebrate their freedom on July 4, Independence Day.

If you were born in July, your lucky flowers are larkspurs and lilies; your lucky gemstone is the ruby.

32

August

Augustus Caesar's month

August is thirty-one days long and is the eighth month of the year. But before the Romans changed their calendar it was the sixth month, so they called it by the name which means sixth, Sextilis. Eight years before Christ was born the name of the month was changed to Augustus in honor of the Roman emperor Augustus Caesar, because many of the important events in his life happened around that time of the year.

The Anglo-Saxons called it *Weod monath*, which means weed month, because it is the month when weeds and other plants grow most rapidly. The name August appears in a play by William Shakespeare, written about 400 years ago. Before then the month was called Augst and Aust.

August is an important month for the winegrowers of Europe, as this proverb from France and Spain tells:

> *When it rains in August it rains honey and wine.*

To people who they feel are becoming over-zealous or too happy, Hindus give this warning:

> *It will not always be August with green fields.*

One of the Hindu forms of god — Krishna — is thought to have been born around August. His birthday is called Janam Ashtami. On Janam Ashtami, Hindus go to their temples to pray and watch people enacting scenes from Krishna's life.

The harvest month

In the Northern Hemisphere August is the time when the grain begins to ripen. Most rhymes and sayings about August are on the harvest theme.

August brings the sheaves of corn.
Then the harvest home is borne.

Shakespeare wrote, in *The Tempest*, of laborers cutting the August corn:

You sun-burned sicklemen, of August weary.

Another poet, who lived at the same time, wrote of August weather:

Dry August and warm
Doth harvest no harm.

Lord Byron was a poet who lived 200 years later, about 1800. He used a reference to August as a way of showing his dislike of British weather:

The English winter — ending in July,
To recommence in August.

August used to be known as Lammas Day, and was Thanksgiving time in Britain and its colonies. The word Lammas comes from an Anglo-Saxon expression, loaf mass. In America people used to bake a loaf from the first sheaves of corn and then take it to the church, where it was blessed. Since 1863, Americans have celebrated Thanksgiving near the end of November (see page 39).

If you were born in August, your lucky flowers are gladioli; your lucky gemstone is the peridot or sardonyx.

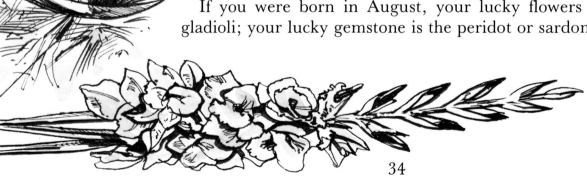

September

The "seventh" month

September is the ninth month of the year and contains thirty days. Its name comes from the old Latin word *septem*, which means seven, because in the Roman calendar it was the seventh month. The Anglo-Saxons called it *Gerst monath* (barley month), because it was the time when they harvested barley to be made into their favorite drink — barley brew. They also called it *Haefest monath*, or harvest month.

Henry VIII, king of England from 1509 to 1547, would probably have known the month by the same name that we do, but before then it was called Septembre and Septembir.

September is the end of the summer in the Northern Hemisphere and the time when fruits begin to ripen. This little rhyme begs the wind not to blow too roughly before the fruit is safely gathered:

> *September blow soft,*
> *'Til the fruit's in the loft.*

It is also harvest time, which is celebrated in towns and villages with special harvest festivals in the churches.

An American poet who lived through most of the nineteenth century was John Greenleaf Whittier. In these two lines he managed to refer to both harvest and climate:

> *Up from the meadows rich with corn,*
> *Clear in the cool September morn.*

The name of the month is given to a hawthorn tree, the September thorn, which is very colorful in parks and

35

gardens in the Northern Hemisphere at this time of year.

An old Hindi proverb issues a stern warning about September:

He will die soon who sleeps on straw in September.

September is the rainy period, so anyone sleeping on straw on the ground would catch a cold.

Hindus celebrate Dasahara (also spelled Dussehra) around this time. On this day one of their forms of god, King Rama, marched against the Ravana, a wicked demon who had stolen his wife. It is customary during the festival for brides and engaged couples to be given presents.

For the Chinese, September is the time of the mid-autumn harvest festival, or moon cake festival. It commemorates the Chinese rebellion against their Mongol rulers 1,000 years ago. Families go to the nearest hill, light lanterns, watch the moon rise, and eat moon cakes and fruit. Americans celebrate Labor Day on the first Monday in September.

If you were born in September, your lucky flowers are asters and your lucky gemstone is the sapphire.

36

October

The "eighth" month

October is the tenth month of the year and is thirty-one days long. The word October comes from the Latin word *octo*, which means eight. It was the eighth month in the old Roman calendar. The Romans wanted to name it after one of their emperors — Antonius, Germanicus, or Herculeus. But it seems that they could not agree which one to choose, so it remained October.

The Anglo-Saxons called it *Win monath*, because it was the month for making wine. They also called it *Winterfylleth* (winter falls) because they believed that winter began with the new moon in October. Before the present spelling of the month was used, it was called Octobre. The French still spell it that way (see chart on pages 44 and 45).

In the West Indies the name October bird is given to the bobolink. The bobolink looks a bit like a finch but is in fact a type of American blackbird. It migrates between North America and Argentina, passing over the Caribbean around October.

October is also the time when animals in the Northern Hemisphere begin to get ready for their winter hibernation. Some Americans believe you can tell how bad the winter will be by the size of wild animals in October:

> *When birds and badgers are fat in October,*
> *Expect a cold winter.*

October festivals

Jewish people hold lots of festivals at this time of year. Rosh Hashanah is the Jewish New Year, which falls in

September or October. For the next ten days Jews think about how well they have spent the past year.

At the end of Rosh Hashanah comes Yom Kippur, the Day of Atonement, which is the most important day in the Jewish calendar. It is the day when Jews fast and confess their sins. When their sins have been forgiven they can begin Sukkot — the Feast of the Tabernacles. Sukkot is a kind of harvest festival which lasts for eight days. It reminds Jews of the hardships their ancestors faced during their wanderings in the wilderness. On the seventh day of the festival people circle the synagogue seven times, holding palm branches, flowering myrtle, and a willow branch in the left hand, and a lemon in the right.

Soon after the end of Sukkot Jewish people celebrate Simhat Torah, the Rejoicing of the Law. The scrolls of Jewish law are carried seven times around the synagogue amid much rejoicing, singing, and dancing.

Hindus also celebrate their new year around this time. The festival of Diwali, also called Festival of Lamps, lasts for up to five days. Presents are exchanged, and every house has a light in the window in the evening. It is said that Vishnu, one of the Hindu forms of god, killed a giant on this day, and women carrying lamps went out to meet him on his return.

Columbus Day, October 12, honors Christopher Columbus and his discovery of America. It is celebrated as a national holiday in the United States and Canada.

If you were born in October your lucky flowers are dahlias and calendulas; your lucky gemstone is the opal.

November

The "ninth" month

November is thirty days long and is the eleventh month of the year. Its name comes from the Latin word *novem,* meaning nine, because it was the ninth month in the Roman calendar. The Roman leaders wanted to name the month after their Emperor Tiberius but he refused. He asked them what they would do when they had used up all the months and the thirteenth emperor came along!

The Anglo-Saxons called November *Wind monath,* because it was the time when the cold winds began to blow. They also called it *Blod monath,* because it was the time when cattle were slaughtered for winter food. King Canute, who ruled England over a thousand years ago, might have called the month Nouember. Later it became Novembre and Nouembre. It was first called November during Shakespeare's time, 400 year ago.

November in the Northern Hemisphere has always been thought of as a gloomy month of mists and frosts. People used to talk of feeling Novemberish or Novembery, meaning miserable. There is a saying that if there is firm ice in November, February will be rainy:

> *If ice in November will bear a duck,*
> *February weather all mire and muck!*

Thanksgiving

November is not all gloom and misery, however. In the United States, Thanksgiving is celebrated near the end of

the month. The first Thanksgiving in America was held by English settlers over 350 years ago. There is a story that ninety friendly Indians gathered around to share the feast, tempted by the smell of roasting turkey. Turkey is still eaten at Thanksgiving today, together with ham, cranberry jelly, mashed potatoes, and yams. This is followed by pumpkin pie, mince pie, and whipped cream. The feast of Thanksgiving is held to praise God for all his blessings.

On the other side of the Pacific, the Japanese hold Seven-Five-Three Festival Day around November. Parents give thanks for the health and well-being of boys ages five and three and girls ages seven and three.

Sikhs celebrate the birthday and life of Guru Nanak. Guru Nanak lived from 1469 to 1533. He founded the religion of Sikhism as a Hindu sect based on the brotherhood of man.

If you were born in November, your lucky flowers are chrysanthemums and your lucky gemstone is the topaz.

December

The ''tenth'' month

December is the twelfth and last month of the year, and is thirty-one days long. It used to be the tenth month of the old Roman year, and it gets its name from the word *decem,* which meant ten. The Romans also described the month as *fumosus*, which means smoky, and *gelidus*, which means frosty.

The Anglo-Saxons called it *Winter monath*, or *Yule monath* because of the custom of burning the yule log around this time. After they were converted to Christianity, they called it *Heligh monath*, which means holy month. In the eleventh century, the month was called Decembris. It was later called Decembre, and finally became December about 500 years ago.

In the Northern Hemisphere December marks the beginning of winter, and in cold countries it is the time of rain, wind, and snow. In his play *Cymbeline*, William Shakespeare says:

> *when we shall hear*
> *The rain and wind beat dark December, how*
> *In this our pinching cave, shall we discourse*
> *The freezing hours away?*

Christmas month

Christians can cheer themselves up during these bleak days by celebrating Christmas. Christmas, the mass of Christ, is held on December 25 and commemorates the birth of Jesus Christ almost 2,000 years ago.

41

Christmas is celebrated in many different ways in countries all over the world. In America and England, families get together to attend church services, sing carols, trade gifts, and eat turkey, mince pies, and other Christmas treats. A fat, jovial man with scarlet clothes and white beard is believed to climb down the chimneys on Christmas night to fill children's stockings with presents. He is called Santa Claus, or Father Christmas. Before Queen Victoria came to the British throne in 1840, Santa Claus was merely the patron saint of German children. Soon after Victoria married a German prince, Santa Claus became associated with Christmas in Britain.

Candles play an important part in the Christmas festivities in Scandinavia. There it is said that the presents are brought by gnomes that live in the attics of houses all year 'round.

In cold Alaska, children wander from house to house carrying a colored star on a long pole and singing carols. In Costa Rica, models of Christ's birthplace in a stable are so big that they fill the room. In Brazil there is folkdancing and singing, and the festivities go on until January 6, which they call Three Kings' Day. January 6 is supposed to be the day when the three wise men visited Jesus to bring him gifts.

Christmas in South Africa and Australia is a summer holiday. However, most people in these countries come from the Northern Hemisphere, or their ancestors did. They cannot quite forget the old winter traditions, and still drape tinsel and cotton wool in shops and houses to look like ice and snow.

Jewish people celebrate Hanukkah, the Festival of Lights. It commemorates the time when the ancient Jews overcame the Syrian hordes. The festival lasts eight days, because it is said that when the Holy Temple was recaptured, a lamp inside which held only one day's supply of oil nevertheless burned for eight days. Hanukkah is a time for giving presents and holding parties.

If you were born in December, your lucky flower is the narcissus; your lucky gemstone is the turquoise.

43

The months around the world

Maart

Martis

When the Roman Empire covered most of Europe, about 2,000 years ago, the use of the Roman names for the months spread to all the countries they colonized. The names were absorbed into the European languages.

Later, between the sixteenth and twentieth centuries, the Spanish, Portuguese, British, French, and other empires spread their languages all over the world. The table on these two pages lists thirteen languages but it covers more than 100 countries.

English is used as the official language, or a very common language, in Australia, Belize, Botswana, Canada,

English	French	Italian	Spanish	Portuguese	Greek
January	Janvier	Gennaio	Enero	Janiero	Yanouarios
February	Fevrier	Febbraio	Febrero	Fevereiro	Fevrouarios
March	Mars	Marzo	Marzo	Marco	Martis
April	Avril	Aprile	Abril	Abril	Apriolios
May	Mai	Maggio	Mayo	Maio	Maios
June	Juin	Giugno	Junio	Junho	Iounios
July	Juillet	Luglio	Julio	Julho	Ioulios
August	Aout	Agosto	Agosto	Agosto	Augoustos
September	Septembre	Settembre	Septiembre	Septembro	Septemvris
October	Octobre	Ottobre	Octubre	Outubro	Octovris
November	Novembre	Novembre	Noviembre	Novembro	Noemvris
December	Decembre	Dicembre	Diciembre	Dezembro	Thekemvris

Eire, Fiji, Ghana, Guyana, Hong Kong, India, Jamaica, Kenya, Malawi, Malaysia, New Zealand, Nigeria, Pakistan, Papua-New Guinea, Philippines, Singapore, South Africa, Sri Lanka, Swaziland, Tanzania, Uganda, the United States, Zambia, and other countries.

French is used similarly in Algeria, Belgium, Benin, Canada, Chad, Congo, Luxembourg, Mali, Niger, Switzerland, Syria, Zaire, and other countries.

Spanish is used similarly in Argentina, Bolivia, Chile, Columbia, Costa Rica, Cuba, Dominican Republic, Ecuador, Guatemala, Honduras, Mexico, Nicaragua, Panama, Paraguay, Peru, Puerto Rico, Venezuela, and other countries.

Portuguese is used similarly in Angola, Brazil, Mozambique, and other countries.

German is used similarly in Austria and Switzerland.

Dutch is the basis of the Afrikaans language used in South Africa.

German	Welsh	Danish	Norwegian	Swedish	Flemish	Dutch
Januar	Ionawr	Januar	Januar	Januari	Januari	Januari
Februar	Chwefror	Februar	Februar	Februari	Februari	Februari
Marz	Mawrth	Marts	Mars	Mars	Maart	Maart
April	Ebrill	April	April	April	April	April
Mai	Mai	Maj	Maia	Maj	Mei	Mei
Juni	Mehefin	Juni	Juni	Juni	Juni	Juni
Juli	Gorffenaf	Juli	Juli	Juli	Juli	Juli
August	Awst	August	August	Augusti	Augustus	August
September	Medi	September	September	September	September	September
Oktober	Hydref	Oktober	Oktober	Oktober	Oktober	Oktober
November	Tachwedd	November	November	November	November	November
Dezember	Rhagfyr	December	Desember	December	December	December

Dutch names for the months

As well as the ordinary names for the months, the Dutch use some beautiful names which describe the climate and the agricultural seasons. These names are very interesting because they are like those used by the Anglo-Saxons more than a thousand years ago.

January	Lauwmaand *(Chilly month)*
February	Sprokelmaand *(Vegetation month)*
March	Lentmaand *(Spring month)*
April	Grasmaand *(Grass month)*
May	Blowmaand *(Flower month)*
June	Zomermaand *(Summer month)*
July	Hooymaand *(Hay month)*
August	Oostmaand *(Harvest month)*
September	Herstmaand *(Autumn month)*
October	Wynmaand *(Wine month)*
November	Slagtmaand *(Slaughter month)*
December	Wintermaand *(Winter month)*

The Hindu year

Most Hindus live in India, but many thousands of them have settled in Britain, the United States, South and East Africa, Canada, and Australia. They use a calendar that is based on twelve lunar months, with an extra month added from time to time to keep the year in line with the solar one.

The names of the months are based on the ancient Hindi names for groups of stars. Each month is named according to the position of the full moon in relation to those stars. The Hindus call those groups of stars naksatras.

The chart below shows the names of the naksatras, the modern Hindi names for the months, and the approximate Gregorian months in which the Hindi months fall.

Naksatra	Hindi name	Gregorian month
Citra	Cait	March-April
Visakha	Baisakh	April-May
Jyestha	Jeth	May-June
Asadha	Asarh	June-July
Sravana	Savan	July-August
Bhadrapada	Bhadom	August-September
Asvini	Asin	September-October
Krttika	Kartik	October-November
Mrgasiras	Margasir	November-December
Pusya	Pus	December-January
Magha	Magh	January-February
Phalguni	Phagun	February-March

The Moslem year

The Moslems revere the prophet Mohammed, who founded their religion in the seventh century. They use a lunar calendar, with no attempt to keep it in line with the solar year. Each year in the Moslem calendar is made up of twelve lunar months of twenty-nine or thirty days. The twelfth month sometimes has an extra day added. The Moslem calendar is used in Iran, Turkey, Arabia, Egypt, Pakistan, and in certain parts of India and Malaya.

1	Muharram *30 days*	5	Jumada I *30 days*	9	Ramadan *30 days*
2	Safar *29 days*	6	Jumada II *29 days*	10	Shawwal *29 days*
3	Rabi I *30 days*	7	Rajab *30 days*	11	Dhu al-Qa'dah *30 days*
4	Rabi II *29 days*	8	Sha'ban *29 days*	12	Dhu al-Hijjah *29 or 30 days*

Because it uses the lunar year, with no "leap" years, the Moslem calendar is always out of step with the Gregorian calendar. The Moslem year moves backward by a few days each year, passing through all seasons, returning to the same point in the solar year every 32½ years.

Seasons

Some of the names given to the months of the modern Moslem calendar come from an old calendar that was adjusted to the solar year. They describe seasonal events. For example, Safar, the second month, comes from the

48

Arabic word ''safara,'' which means ''to become empty.'' In the old Moslem calendar this month fell at the time of year when the granaries became empty.

Rabi, the name given to the third and fourth months, describes the season late in the year when the earth becomes green again after the autumn rains. Jumada, the name given to the fifth and sixth months, probably comes from ''jamada,'' which means to become hard or to freeze. In the old Moslem calendar these months obviously fell in winter. Ramadan, the ninth month, gets its name from ''ramada,'' which means to be heated by the sun. This month probably fell in the middle of summer.

Holy days

Not all the names of the Moslem months are connected with the seasons, though. The eleventh month, Dhu al-Qa'dah, means ''owner of the truce'' in Arabic. Traditionally, this was the time when the Arabs waged no warfare. Dhu al-Hijjah means ''owner of the pilgrimage.'' It is the time when Moslems from all over the world make a journey to the holy city of Mecca.

Ramadan is another very religious month. It is a period of fasting, and for the whole month, food, drink, and smoking are forbidden between daybreak and sundown. Muharram, the first month, means ''sacred'' in Arabic and is another time of fasting. For ten days Moslems fast in mourning for the death of Hasain, Mohammed's grandson. They commemorate the death of Mohammed himself on the twelfth day of Rabi I, in a festival called Barah Wafat. In the month before, Safar, they celebrate the festival of Akhiri-Chahar Shamba. This commemorates the day near the end of Mohammed's life when he recovered enough to bathe himself. Today, Moslems write out seven blessings, then wash off the ink and drink it.

49

The Jewish year

Jewish people live not only in Israel, but in countries all over the world. Their calendar is "lunisolar," like the Hindu calendar (see page 47). The months are lunar and are twenty-nine or thirty days long. But the years are solar, like the Gregorian year. Because the lunar year of twelve months only amounts to 354 days, an extra month is added to the Jewish year seven times in nineteen years. In this way, the third, sixth, eighth, eleventh, fourteenth, seventeenth, and nineteenth years are thirteen months long. The extra month brings the Jewish year into line with the Gregorian year. The Jewish New Year always falls around September, and the calendar looks like this:

1	Tishri	6	Adar	9	Sivan
	30 days		*29 or 30 days*		*30 days*
2	Heshvan		Adar Sheni*	10	Tammuz
	29 or 30 days		*29 days*		*29 days*
3	Kislev	7	Nisan	11	Av
	29 or 30 days		*30 days*		*30 days*
4	Tevet	8	Iyyar	12	Elul
	29 days		*29 days*		*29 days*
5	Shevat				
	30 days		*only in leap years*		

Babylonian and Assyrian months

About 600 years before Christ was born, the Jews were taken into exile by the Babylonians. Several of the modern names for the Jewish months come from the names that the Babylonians gave to their months. In turn, some of the names that the Babylonians gave to their months come from Assyrian words. The Assyrians were a tribe who ruled the Middle East about 3,000 years ago. Therefore, the names of the Jewish months are very ancient indeed.

Heshvan may come from the Assyrian word "Arahsammu." Arahsammu was the name for the eighth month in the Assyrian calendar, which probably fell at around the same time as Heshvan. Adar is thought to come from Adrammelech, the son of the great Assyrian King Sennacherib. Nisan comes from the Babylonian word "Nisannu," which means to start. The first month in the Babylonian calendar was called Nisannu. Kislev, Shevat, and Elul are all ancient Babylonian or Assyrian words.

The name of the first month, Tishri, comes from the Syrian word "shera," or "sherei," which means to begin. Tevet may take its name from "tava," which means to sink in. Tevet falls around December, which is a wet and muddy time. The name of the eighth month, Iyyar, may come from the Hebrew word "or," which means light. Iyyar falls in springtime in the Northern Hemisphere and is the time when the days get longer and brighter.

The Chinese year

The Chinese calendar is probably one of the oldest, and is both lunar and solar. Although it is no longer officially used in China itself, except in Tibet, Chinese people living in Hong Kong, Singapore, and Malaysia still use it. There are many Chinese also living in countries like the United States, Britain, Canada, and Australia who use the old calendar for religious affairs.

The lunar calendar is composed of twelve lunar months. These can be either big months, which are thirty days long, or small months of twenty-nine days. The months are simply numbered one to twelve. An extra month, called something like 6a, is added from time to time to keep the lunar year in line with the solar year.

The solar calendar is used jointly with the lunar calendar. Its main use is to help people to organize agriculture, and it is divided into twenty-four solar periods. Each period is called a *chieh* and is almost 15¼ days long. The names of the solar periods describe the state of the weather or agriculture at that time of year. The chart opposite shows when the solar periods fall in a Gregorian year.

52

February 5th	The Spring Begins
February 19th	The Rain Water
March 5th	The Excited Insects
March 21st	The Vernal Equinox
April 5th	The Clear and Bright
April 20th	The Grain Rains
May 5th	The Summer Begins
May 21st	The Grain Fills
June 6th	The Grain in Ear
June 21st	The Summer Solstice
July 7th	The Slight Heat
July 23rd	The Great Heat
August 7th	The Autumn Begins
August 27th	The Limit of Heat
September 8th	The White Dew
September 23rd	The Autumn Equinox
October 8th	The Cold Dew
October 23rd	The Hoar Frost Descends
November 7th	The Winter Begins
November 22nd	The Little Snow
December 7th	The Heavy Snow
December 22nd	The Winter Solstice
January 6th	The Little Cold
January 20th	The Severe Cold

The sun signs

For thousands of years people have believed that the position of the sun, moon, and planets at the time of a person's birth is very important. It is supposed to decide what sort of person they are, and what will happen to them at important periods of their life. This belief is still a serious part of Indian and Chinese religions. Young people will not marry if their "stars" seem to tell them that they would not suit each other.

Astrology, as it is called, is not taken quite so seriously by people in most western countries. Magazines which print "star predictions" expect most people to read them mainly for fun.

An important part of astrology is the system of sun signs. The position of the sun at the moment of birth is supposed to have a very strong influence on character. The sun has twelve main positions, which are given special names. It stays in each position for about one month. Even if you don't believe in astrology, it's quite fun to see how accurate your sun sign is. Look at the dates below and find where your birthday falls. See if you agree with the description of yourself or of your friends.

March 21st to April 20th (Aries)

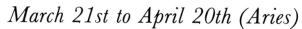

If you are an Aries person you are strong-willed, stubborn, and demanding. You will get angry if you don't get your own way, but your anger never lasts very long, and you are very affectionate. You probably *hate* doing homework even more than everyone else does! If you are challenged in your school work, you can do very well. You take the lead over your friends and with your vivid imagination you are always inventing new games and new things to do. You love books, especially those about brave, shining heroes. The symbol for Aries is the Ram.

April 21st to May 21st (Taurus)

If you were born when the sun was in Taurus you are stubborn. You hate being pushed around or teased, or being made the center of attention. You are very lovable, though, and adore being cuddled, hugged, squeezed, and petted. You are probably strong and healthy and love sports and games. You are not easily ruffled and never show off. Taurus people are often musical and like to draw, color, and paint. In school, you work hard and are good at tests. The symbol for Taurus is the Bull.

May 22nd to June 21st (Gemini)

If you are a Gemini, there is a higher than average chance that you will have a twin brother or sister. You will grow up quickly and are very inquisitive, active, and quick thinking. You are always fidgeting and wanting to do three or four things at once. You are often doing your homework and listening to the radio at the same time! You are bright and interesting, you learned to read easily, and you always enjoy sharing what you know with other people. You are good with your hands and can probably use both of them equally well. This makes you good at doing magic tricks and playing musical instruments. You like to learn foreign languages because you talk and travel a lot. You find it difficult to arrive anywhere on time. The symbol for Gemini is the Twins.

June 22nd to July 23rd (Cancer)

If you are a Cancer person your moods will change very quickly. You can be very sensitive, and if upset you will cry rivers of tears. You may be shy and like playing on your own, often inventing imaginary playmates. But you love being cuddled and adored. You are artistic and creative and at school your amazing memory will help you in history, where you'll remember dates and events with ease. You like to earn money doing odd jobs, and you love telling jokes. The symbol for Cancer is the Crab.

July 24th to August 23rd (Leo)

If you are a Leo, you delight in being the leader and tend to sulk when you're not. You are sunny, happy, playful, and jolly — all the time you're getting your own way! You are sometimes bossy and proud, and you like to show off and do reckless things. You love a challenge and enjoy having the chance to explain something to somebody else. At school you learn fast, but are sometimes very lazy. The symbol for Leo is the Lion.

August 24th to September 23rd (Virgo)

If you are a Virgo, you are alert and quick but at the same time you like peace and calm. You are honest and always pay careful attention to detail. You are a fussy eater but neat and tidy. You hate having your belongings moved or your privacy invaded, and always follow your own personal schedules. At school you may well be teacher's pet because you study hard and are easy to discipline. You are always asking why. You love small animals and insects. The symbol for Virgo is the Virgin.

September 24th to October 23rd (Libra)

If the sun was in Libra when you were born you will always hate having to make decisions, particularly in a hurry. You like to seek after the truth, are kind and fair, but hate making mistakes and are usually very cautious. You like to play hard and then relax hard too, and are often accused of laziness as a result! You probably love sweets. You hate getting out of the bath. You have charming manners and are often spoiled. At school you are neat, musical, and artistic, and teachers will like you because you have a bright and logical mind. The symbol for Libra is the Scales.

October 24th to November 22nd (Scorpio)

If you are a Scorpio, then your parents and teachers had better beware! You are strong willed and strong bodied, and you need firm discipline. You like to say exactly what you think, and are often sarcastic. You like a good fight, which you usually win, and can bear pain without crying. You are loyal to your friends and to your loved ones, but hard on everyone else! At school you learn quickly and tend to be the leader in school activities. You love Halloween, monster films, science fiction, and ghost stories. You like to get what you want, but are brave, and intelligent. The symbol for Scorpio is the Scorpion.

November 23rd to December 21st (Sagittarius)

If you are a Sagittarian you are remarkably honest, happy-go-lucky, playful, and affectionate. You hate being told what to do by teachers or parents unless you understand and accept the reasoning behind the order. You are always asking questions and demanding answers. Your curiosity will help you at school although you may be bored by authority. You are amazingly clumsy and awkward although you never cheat. You are probably interested in religion. The symbol for Sagittarius is the Archer, shown as a Centaur.

December 22nd to January 20th (Capricorn)

If you were born with the sun in Capricorn you are strong willed and know what you like. You rarely throw tantrums if people annoy you, but prefer to make your tormenters look foolish. You love schedules and routines and always know exactly where you have put things. You like the home life and never have large gangs of friends. You learn slowly at school, but tend to do well. Although you are often bossed around you are quite capable of looking after yourself, and always get your own back somehow. The symbol for Capricorn is the Goat, shown with a fish's tail.

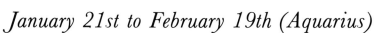

January 21st to February 19th (Aquarius)

If your sun sign is Aquarius you are probably stubborn, good at inventing things, impulsive, and quick thinking. It is often difficult for people around you to know exactly what you are going to do next. You are lovable and often amusing, but always day-dreaming and forgetting where you have put things. In class, you are often caught looking out of the window instead of paying attention! It can be hard to interest you in sports, for you probably prefer natural things like birds, trees and the seashore. The symbol for Aquarius is the Water Carrier.

February 20th to March 20th (Pisces)

If you are a Pisces person you like to live in a world of fantasy and make-believe, far removed from reality. You love books like *Peter Pan* and *Alice in Wonderland*. You hate organization and routines and prefer to work when you want to, play when you want to, and eat when you want to. You probably throw a tantrum every time you don't get your way! You love attention and affection. You find school difficult because of the routine, and your favorite subjects will be art, music, and dancing rather than science. You are probably a good storyteller. The symbol for Pisces is a pair of Fish.

Glossary

Aborigine One of the original black inhabitants of Australia.

Babylonians An ancient race of people who lived in the Euphrates Valley, now a part of Iraq.

calendar A system of measuring the passing of the years, and parts of years.

Catholic A Christian who believes the Pope is God's representative on earth.

Christian A follower of the religion founded in the first century by Jesus Christ.

day The time taken by the earth to rotate once on its own axis.

Easter An annual festival on a Sunday in March or April which commemorates the death and rebirth of Jesus Christ.

Gregorian calendar The reformed Julian calendar introduced by Pope Gregory in 1583, which leaves out the leap year in any centennial year not divisible by 4. Thus 1900 was not a leap year, but 2000 will be.

Hindu A follower of the Hindu religion, the main religion of India, which worships many forms of God and believes in reincarnation.

Jesus Christ The Jewish founder of the Christian religion. Christians believe he is the son of God, and that three days after being executed he came to life again to live in Heaven. The calendar used in most countries dates from the year of his birth.

Jew A follower of the Jewish religion, descended from the Hebrews of Biblical times who lived in the country now called Israel.

Julian calendar The calendar introduced by Julius Caesar in 46 B.C. which fixed the year at 365 days with an extra day every fourth year (leap year).

Julius Caesar The great soldier and dictator of the Romans who founded the Julian calendar.

leap year A year containing 366 days, a February 29 being added to keep the calendar years in line with the solar years.

lunar Anything to do with the moon – of or about the moon, or resembling the moon.

lunar year A year measured by moons or months; that is, the time it takes for the moon to change from old to new twelve times, which is about 354 days.

month The approximate time taken by the moon to make one orbit of the earth.

Moslem A follower of the Moslem religion founded by Mohammed in Arabia in the seventh century.

Northern Hemisphere The half of the earth between the Equator and the North Pole, where midwinter is in December and midsummer in June. The seasons are the opposite in the Southern Hemisphere.

Orthodox Church The Christian Church

of eastern Europe and western Asia which does not accept the authority of the Pope, who is head of the Catholic Church.

Passover An annual Jewish festival in late March or early April commemorating the Jews' liberation from slavery in Egypt.

Romans The ancient race of people who had their capital at Rome, and established an empire covering much of Europe, northern Africa, and the Middle East.

Sikh A follower of the Sikh religion founded by Guru Nanak in northwestern India in the sixteenth century.

solar year The exact time it takes for the earth to make one orbit of the sun — 365.242199 days.

synagogue A Jewish church.

Thanksgiving An annual festival on the fourth Thursday in November in the United States and Canada commemorating the first harvest of the early settlers, and thanking God for his blessings.

year The time taken by the earth to make one orbit of the sun. For the sake of the Gregorian calendar this is regarded as 365 or 366 days.

Index

62